OSCAR NIEMEYER

© 2002 Assouline Publishing for the present edition
601 West 26th Street, 18th floor
New York, NY 10001
USA
Tel.: 212 989-6810   Fax: 212 647-0005
www.assouline.com

First published by Editions Assouline, Paris, France.

Translated from the French by Charles Penwarden
Copyedited by Margarte Burnham

Color separation: Gravor (Switzerland)
Printed by Grafiche Milani (Italy)

ISBN: 2 84323 344 5

OSCAR NIEMEYER

MATTHIEU SALVAING

ASSOULINE

You ask me to talk about my architecture, about my life, about what gives me pleasure or makes me sad. And I am going to try to satisfy you with a few short words, to say that the important thing is not architecture, which for sixty years has kept me at my drawing board. For me, the important things are life, friends, and this unjust world that we must make better.

I do only what appeals to me, quite freely, convinced as I am that architecture is above all a matter of invention. Moreover, I believe in intuition, and see architectural creation as something very personal that you cannot teach or learn. Each architect must have his own architecture.

As for life, I always say that, sadly, I am a pessimist, and see human beings as fragile, abandoned and with no hope. Still, life has to be lived, and since we're all in the same boat, we must live it hand in hand, together.

The rest is time, and we follow it irremediably. Happy when times are good, women pretty, friends fraternal and the sky blue and starry. Sad and outraged when life becomes cruel, when misery spreads and our poorest brothers are forsaken and left to despair.

When hope deserts men's hearts, revolution surely follows.

I definitely believe in human intelligence, and that one day we will be flying through the cosmos, chatting with our brothers in space, yet still asking the same anxious question: "But who are we?"

Oscar Niemeyer, October 2001

You belong to a small group of Brazilians who have international recognition. Does that gratify you?

There is a certain exaggeration there. I'm just a man like any other. I worked, I was lucky, I had help, I had opportunities and I made the most of them. That's all. I worked very hard. I spent my life bending over the drawing board. But I don't regret that. I always saved some time for the most important things, like reading, looking after my family, living with my friends, always bearing in mind that life is more important than architecture. As I get older, I try to adapt myself. I am a pessimist; I can't see much future for human beings. And I try to live a calm life, to do what I like, to protest, to struggle against poverty and search for a better world.

It's curious that your first work, Obra do Berço, is a kind of hospital.

It wasn't a hospital, but a small charity run by my cousin Lísia Sodré, who asked me to do the project. A modest work, with little significance in my architectural career. For me, my architecture begins in Pampulha, Minas Gerais.

Is it really in Pampulha that the architect Oscar Niemeyer comes into focus?

Pampulha was the starting point of this freer architecture full of curves which I still love even today. It was, in fact, the beginning of Brasilia, with a very special peculiarity: it's the first work that JK [Juscelino Kubitschek] built as a public figure, my first important project and the first construction by my friend Marco Paulo Rabello, who also made a remarkable contribution to Brasilia, all the way through to the end. Of course, like all the architects of my generation, I was influenced by Le Corbusier, but that didn't prevent my architecture from going in a different direction, which is something he always understood and praised. "There is invention here," he said to Italo Campofiorito when walking up the ramp of the National Congress.

Le Corbusier, one of your few influences, is generally rectilinear, like in the Ministry of Education and Health headquarters. There are some exceptions, like the chapel at Ronchamp…

Ronchamp Chapel… That, they say, marks the beginning of my influence on that architect's work, which naturally pleases me very much.

What do you think of Brazilian architecture today?

Of course we have great architects, but when I walk around some streets in Brasilia or when I go to Barra da Tijuca, I feel that there's still too much mediocrity around.

Have you been to Barra da Tijuca lately? What would you say about it? Is that architecture?

I don't like Barra. It looks like Miami, a Miami suburb, and worse, there's even a copy of the Statue of Liberty there, oppressing us somehow. Everywhere mediocrity and the power of the state are being imposed on us.

But that is typical of Brazilian cities. In Europe, city centers were kept more or less intact, despite the wars. A Roman from the nineteenth century or even from the Renaissance would still recognize a good part of his city today... In Rio, transformations are brutal. The beautiful sights that were around when I was a teenager are no longer there to be seen.

When modern architecture and urbanism appeared, Paris already had a defined architectural style, and its people have always been concerned with its preservation. That's what we miss in Rio.

Here, in places like Avenida Rio Branco, we have had five generations of buildings in only a century...

But you've got to consider that, when modern architecture arrived in Rio, it didn't find, as it did in Europe, an architecture that was already established and impossible to despise, which could impose some discipline on it.

But the annihilation of Pereira Passos' work... Old Avenida Central was a pastiche, but it was a monument in the city's history, with buildings imitating France, even Buenos Aires, a neo-something...

When Le Corbusier was here, he congratulated Pereira Passos for the construction of that avenue, despite the inevitable demolition.

There are some who say that your mark is much more that of a sculptor than of an architect. What do you think?

It's not easy to elaborate the kind of architecture that I like, in which courage and plastic freedom are essential. But for that, you need to know how to draw—including figuratively. And to understand how important surprise and invention are.

This freedom must be the engineer's nightmare, don't you think?

On the contrary. All the engineers who worked with me, like Emilio

Baumgart, Joaquim Cardozo, Bruno Contarini, Fernando Souza and Jose Carlos Sussekind, have always taken pleasure in calculating my structures. Even in Italy, the great Italian engineer Riccardo Moranzi, who was in charge of the calculations for the FATA headquarters, once declared in one of his books: "For the first time in my life I've got to put into practice everything I know about reinforced concrete." This proves that my imagination helps techniques to evolve.

The idea is worthy of a Renaissance architect!
In those days, there was at least a certain grandeur, and everybody was trying to achieve beauty. Artists and architects could do whatever they wanted, provided they managed their powerful patrons properly. The Doge's Palace in Venice, designed by the architect Calendario, is the real precursor of today's architecture. It is, to my point of view, more genuine architecture than what was built centuries later in accordance with the dogmas of the Bauhaus, and by the group of architects who put them into practice.
In that project, Calendario contests so-called architectonic simplicity with a beautiful structure covered with arches and curves that contrast with the building's plain walls. The same applies to the economy of construction. Since, like me, he was dealing with large, open spaces, he covered the 55-yards span of the main hall with a simple latticework. He even gives a hint of the lighter architecture that I prefer, with the columns seemingly standing free of the building, down by the sea. He also frees himself from absolute functionalism by creating architectonic elements that are dispensable, but that, from his point of view, were necessary for its beauty. This is freedom asserting itself, the same freedom that JK gave me in Brasilia and that a stranger from Norway offered when he said: "I want a house with three suites. Here is the site plan. The rest is

up to you. I will write a book about this house." He was no fool. He was a friend of Brecht's and lived with Sartre for four years in Paris. He's a writer, a curator in an important museum. He recently told me over the phone: "The house is beautiful! We're going to start the building work."

The 20th century, with all its suffering, was not the best period for an ordinary person. But think what it was like to be an ordinary man in the 1st, 16th or 17th century...
Yes. There is always some progress, or rather, we should say that the suffering makes it necessary.

Perhaps Oscar Niemeyer wouldn't have been possible then. Of course in the 15th or 16th century, if you were in Florence, and with your talent, you would have been Bramante, Michelangelo or someone like that. But in the 20th century, you were able to make Brasilia.
I've done so much work that, for me, Brasilia is just a phase within these long years in which I occupied myself with architecture, carrying my own personal way of conceiving it abroad. But Brasilia was important. JK's great adventure today is fairly well justified by the progress that, as he hoped it would, is spreading all around the interior of the country. I visited Goiania when Brasilia was being built—a small town of no importance. A few days ago, I was amazed when I saw that it is full of new buildings, squares and gardens! And all that was made possible by the President's enthusiasm, by Israel Pinheiro, who sorted out all the problems by Lucio Costa and to all those who enthusiastically collaborated in its realization.

Something very intriguing is going on in Brazil nowadays: more than 80% of Brazilians now live in cities.
It's to solve this problem that our landless brothers are fighting for

agrarian reform, for the land that belonged to them long ago—a very important movement that will be able to solve this rural exodus that you mentioned. And it's worth remembering Stédile's courage as its leader, linking it to the struggle against poverty, which is the cause of all the evils that still exist in this country.

Is there any work you would like to have done and for some reason haven't?
From the architectonic point of view, I would like to see the mosque that I designed for Algiers.

And of all the buildings you have designed, is there any special one? One which has marked your life?
In Brazil, the National Congress and the Niterói Museum of Contemporary Art. Abroad, the Mondadori headquarters and the University at Constantine in Algeria. They are different and surprising, and that's important in architecture.

Even in architecture, you have to put into practice the concept that man has a right to beauty. It makes people's lives better. There is a very beautiful thing in the preface of the American Constitution, where it says that God created man with some inalienable rights, such as life, freedom and the pursuit of happiness. How would you define happiness? You said you left a party where people were happy, for no particular reason. But what makes you happy?
To be at peace, at ease with myself. To feel solidarity with those who are fighting against oppression and poverty. And to help other people. I think we must have pleasure in helping one another, that's what's important. And not doing it because it's an obligation. When I'm walking down the street and someone asks me for money, if I have some, I give it—it doesn't matter whether it's for drinking or

not. It's a pleasurable moment that I like to be able to offer. I love to invite my poorer friends to travel to Europe with me and see how happy they are exploring the "Old World"!

You said that Rodrigo M.F. de Andrade encouraged you to write. Your designs always have a "necessary explanation" and your texts have real literary quality.
I have to explain. In most cases, my designs are approved on the strength of their texts, not their drawings. And if, while I'm writing, I feel a lack of convincing arguments, I go back to the drawing board. It's my acid test.

What do you think about, for instance, when you design a church?
I think of the people who go there to pray, those who believe in God. In the cathedral at Brasilia, I put some transparent spaces in the stained glass, so that from the nave the believers could imagine that out there, in the infinite spaces, the Lord would be waiting for them—a new idea that a representative of the Pope enthusiastically approved when traveling through Brasilia.

You do design beautiful churches!
For me, when architecture is not beautiful and does not amaze, it doesn't assume the characteristics of a genuine work of art. And thus, drawing is essential for the architect, including figurative drawing, which they have started to replace with technology and computers in schools. A talented 8- or 10-year-old can produce fantastic drawings that bad teaching and the knowledge of the classics will make hopelessly vulgar.

Isn't that rather what Picasso was striving for? When he said he would like to paint with the freedom of a child... Another question

that has nothing to do with that… At what point in your life did you commit to the Left?
It was when I understood the immense scale of poverty and that I had to fight it.

But, in a way, isn't it true that when you are writing a book or designing a building you have to be transported to its interior in order to imagine it? In the creative process, it's not only intellectual satisfaction that counts. There must be something from the soul in there. By "soul" I mean this flame that keeps man alive.
And that happens at the moment of creation, when the architect, as Machado de Assis did so well, penetrates the soul of those who will use his architecture.

Now, back to "immortality" in quotation marks, isn't it nice for you to know that, even after your death, people will look at your buildings and say: "Wow, what a building!"
It's true. That may happen for a while. But afterwards… Still, it's nature's law, eternally repeated, implacable.

Interview by Fritz Utzeri.

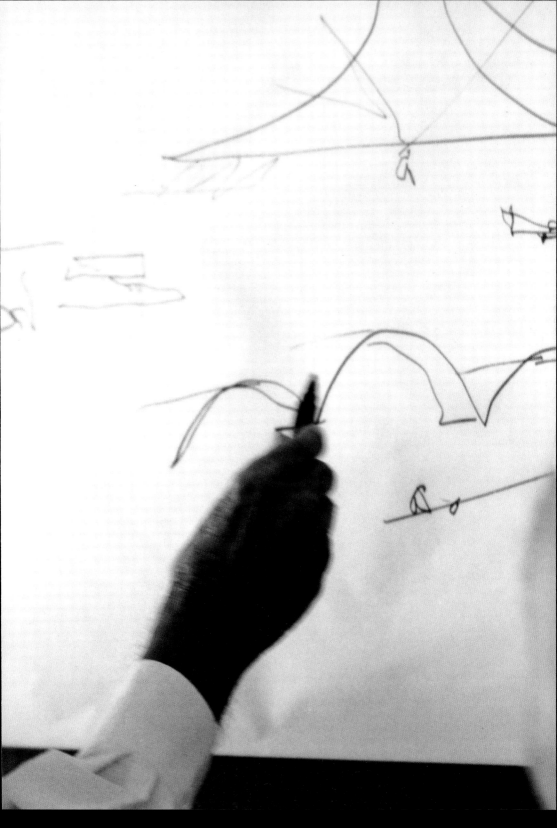

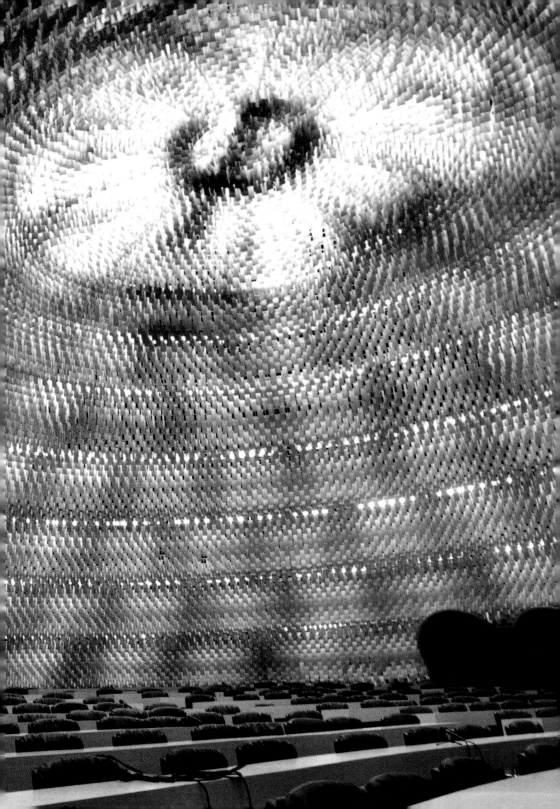

Chronology

1907:	Born in Rio de Janeiro on December 15.
1922:	Enrolled at Santa Antonio Maria Zaccaria Priory School, Rio, run by Barnabite priests.
1928:	Leaves school. Marries Annita Baldo.
1929:	Studies at the National School of Fine Arts, Rio.
1934:	Graduates with a BA in architecture.
1935:	Works in the offices of architects Lucio Costa and Carlos Leao.
1936:	Is part of the Costa and Leao team designing the Ministry of Education and Health building in Rio. Meets Le Corbusier and Gustavo Capanema.
1937:	Designs the Obra do Berço in Rio.
1939:	Travels to New York with Lucio Costa to design the Brazilian Pavilion at the World's Fair.
1940:	Meets Juscelino Kubitschek, then mayor of Belo Horizonte, who commissions him to design the Pampulha complex.
1945:	Joins the Brazilian Communist Party.
1946:	Invited to teach at Yale as a visiting professor, but is refused a visa for the United States.
1947:	Having finally obtained a visa, Niemeyer travels to New York to design the United Nations building.
1950:	Publication in the U.S. of *The Work of Oscar Niemeyer*, by Stamo Papadaki.
1951:	Designs the Ibirapuera Park complex and the Copan building in São Paulo.
1952:	Designs his own house on Estrada dos Canoas (no. 2310), Rio.
1954:	Makes his first trip to Europe to take part in the postwar reconstruction program.
1955:	Founds the journal *Modulo* in Rio de Janeiro. Made director of the architecture department at NOVACAP, the government authority set up to build the new capital at Brasilia.
1956:	Made responsible for organizing the competition for a master plan for Brasilia. He is also a member of the jury.
1957–1958:	Designs Brasilia's presidential residence (Palacio da Alvorada) and other main buildings.
1961:	Publishes *Minha Experiencia em Brasilia* (My Experience in Brasilia).
1962:	Appointed coordinator of the School of Architecture at the newly created Brasilia University-UnB. Travels to Lebanon to design the Rachid Karami permanent exhibition center in Tripoli.
1963:	Made an honorary member of the American Institute of Architects.
1964:	When traveling in Israel, is surprised by news of the coup d'état in Brazil. Returns in November and is summoned by the political police (DOPS) for official opposition to the regime. Elected to the American Academy of Arts and Letters.
1965:	Resigns from Brasilia University along with two hundred other faculty members in protest against university policies imposed by the regime. Travels to Paris for the opening of the Niemeyer retrospective at the Musée des Arts Décoratifs. Publishes his *Texts and Drawings for Brasilia*.
1966:	Publishes *Viagens: Quase Memorias*.
1967:	Unable to work in Brazil, he decides to settle in Paris.

The Art Deco building on Avenida Atlantica housing Niemeyer's offices at Copacabana, Rio de Janeiro.

1968:	Commissioned to design the head office for publishers Mondadori in Milan, Italy, and plans several projects for Algiers (university, mosque and government buildings).
1969:	Commissioned to design Constantine University, Algeria.
1970:	Resigns from the American Academy of Arts and Letters in protest against the war in Vietnam. In Paris, he has an office on the Champs-Elysées. Travels around Europe, following a touring exhibition of his work.
1975:	Designs the Fata-European Group headquarters in Turin, Italy. Mondadori publishes *Oscar Niemeyer*. In Rio, the journal *Modulo* resumes publication.
1978:	Co-founder of Centro Brazil Democratico CEBRADE (Democratic Brazil Center), of which he is elected first president. Retrospective exhibition, Niemeyer, at the Pompidou Center, Paris.
1983:	Retrospective at the Museu de Arte Moderna, Rio.
1985:	Goes back to designing projects for Brasilia.
1987–1988:	Wins the Pritzker Prize for Architecture (Chicago, USA). Designs the Memorial to Latin America at São Paulo.
1990:	Leaves the Brazilian Communist Party, along with Luiz Carlos Prestes.
1991:	Designs the Museu de Arte Contemporanea, Niterói (Rio).
1993:	Publication of his *Conversa da Arquiteto*.
1994:	Designs plans for the Museo do Homem o seu Universo (Museum of Man and His Universe) in Brasilia, and the Embratel Tower in Rio.
1995:	Designs the monument celebrating the centennial of Belo Horizonte. Made Doctor Honoris Causa by the universities of São Paulo and Minas Gerais.
1996:	Designs the Eldorado-Memoria monument, which he donates to the Landless Rural Workers' Movement. Awarded the Golden Lion at the sixth international architecture show held concurrently with the Venice Biennale.
1997:	Preliminary plans for Avenida Niemeyer at Niteroi (Rio); Museu de Arte Moderna, Brasilia; TECNET (technology center of Americana City Hall), São Paulo. Riocentro convention center, Rio de Janeiro. Exhibitions are held around Brazil to celebrate his 90th birthday.
1998:	Awarded the Gold Medal by the Royal Institute of British Architects. Preliminary drawings for the Santa Helena cultural center, Parana; Architectural complex of memorial and residence of Ulysses Guimaraes at Rio Claro (São Paulo); Darcy Ribeiro Memorial at Sambrodromo (Rio de Janeiro); Maria Aragao memorial at São Luis do Maranhao. Touros monument and permanent creche at Natal (Rio Grande do Norte).
1999:	Projects include designs for a new theater for the Ibirapuera Park at São Paulo, the cultural district of Brasilia, the administrative center at Betim (Minas Gerais) and the monument for the 500th anniversary of the discovery of Brazil at São Vicente (São Paulo). Exhibition of Niemeyer's *Sculptures* at the Niteroi contemporary art museum.
2000:	Modulo Educaçao Integrada-MEI (General Studies Department), a day center of the CIEP (Popular Research and Education Center), administrative center for Goiania, Cassiano Ricardo Memorial at São José dos Campos (São Paulo), headquarters of the National Students' Union at Rio, auditorium at Ravello, Italy.

Memorial to Latin America, São Paulo, Brazil, 1986–1988.

Oscar Niemeyer

Oscar Niemeyer in his office in New York. © Archives Fundaçao Oscar Niemeyer. **National Congress,** Brasilia, 1958. The Palacio do Planalto, the Supreme Court and the Congress are the main buildings on Three Powers Square. Its privileged location, at the end of the perspective along the monumental axis, necessitated a building capable of communicating its strength over considerable distances. The office towers stand out as notable landmarks in the cityscape.

Pantheon of Freedom and Democracy, Brasilia, 1985. Also known as the Pantheon of Tancredo Neves, it stands on Three Powers Square and draws its expressive strength from its two huge white "wings" in reinforced concrete.

Cathedral of Nossa Senhora Aparecida (Our Lady of the Apparition), Brasilia, 1959–1970. Niemeyer was looking for a pure, compact form that, whatever the angle from which it was seen, would express a deep religious feeling. The slightly tinted, heat-resistant glass was inserted into a fine metal mesh in 1970, thus conserving the lightness and transparency of the whole.

Supreme Court, Brasilia, 1958–1960. On a platform that seems to float above the ground, the building aims for a natural fusion of space and architecture. Any visual obstacle that might be confused with the line of the horizon is excluded. The cleverly calculated use of perspective is such that the pillars do not mask one another, whatever the angle from which the building is viewed.

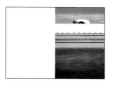

Juscelino Kubitschek Memorial, Brasilia, 1980–1981. Housing the tomb of the eponymous founder of Brasilia and a museum, this structure stands on the monumental axis. The meditative, intimate feeling inside is heightened by the limited amount of light, which is restricted to what passes under the lens-shaped concrete roof.

Juscelino Kubitschek Memorial, Brasilia, 1980–1981. The Kubitschek Museum. Niemeyer first met the then Mayor of Belo Horizonte in 1940, when the latter commissioned him to design the new peripheral quarter of Pampulha. This first project would lead to international recognition for his work on Brasilia, commissioned when Kubitschek became President of the Republic in 1956.

Chairs and stools designed by Oscar Niemeyer, here in the National Congress building. The architect only began designing furniture late in his career, conceiving his first chairs during his Paris sojourn in 1972. His approach grew directly out of his architectural concerns: each material was to be raised to the perfection allowed by its structural limits.

Museu de Arte Contemporanea, Brasilia, 1981–1988. Initially planned as a museum of the Indian population, the building had a circular plan with an open roof at the center endowing the ensemble with great luminosity. The facade, in which the entrance is the only opening, contrasts with the open inner courtyard overlooked by the exhibition rooms.

National Congress, Brasilia, 1958. This building houses the National Assembly and the Senate. This dual function is expressed in the architecture, with the long horizontal line of the parliament broken by the block of offices, on each side of which the two cupolas, the Assembly (right) and the Senate (left) seem like a natural extension of Three Powers Square.

Yacht Club, Pampulha-Belo Horizonte, Brazil, 1940. The attractive rhythm of the facade (seen here from inside) is the result of careful positioning of the canopies.
Justice Ministry, Brasilia, 1962. An example of the felicitous formula worked out by Niemeyer for the main public buildings in Brasilia. Here, the arcades and waterspouts reflected in the water outside the building set up an association between the visual forms and the murmur of the water.

Oscar Niemeyer at Copacabana, Rio de Janeiro, November 2000. "I have always loved drawing. In this sense, I have always thought with my hands."

Church of Sao Francisco de Asis (Saint Francis of Assisi), Pampulha-Belo Horizonte, 1940. Two large parabolic vaults envelop the nave and main altar, dominating an ensemble that is itself articulated in a series of vaults. The canopy over the entrance and the bell tower stand out as elements of a different order.

Church of Sao Francisco de Asis (Saint Francis of Assisi), Pampulha-Belo Horizonte, 1940. Niemeyer's language here is different from that in the other buildings at Pampulha. Instead of transparency, he opts for an opaque structure using new forms, creating an atmosphere conducive to meditation inside.

Art museum (originally a casino), Pampulha-Belo Horizonte, Brazil, 1940–1942. The casino was the first building Niemeyer designed for Pampulha. The use of floating ramps to connect the different levels plays on contrasting heights and, in the absence of visual barriers, facilitates the interplay of interior and exterior.

Art museum (originally a casino: auditorium), Pampulha-Belo Horizonte, Brazil, 1940–1942. While the perfect geometry of the auditorium does not clearly express its main purpose, there remains the harmony between the symbolism of the circle and the room's entertainment function.

Casa do Baile (dance hall), Pampulha-Belo Horizonte, Brazil, 1940. Here, Niemeyer made use of water as an architectonic element for the first time. This would become a recurrent characteristic of his work. The horizontal plane of the roof is continued out over the water's edge by a canopy, inspired by the outline of the island on which the Casa do Baile stands.

Praça Liberdade apartment building, Belo Horizonte, 1954–1960. The privileged site, one of the highest parts of the city, allowed Niemeyer to give free rein to his imagination. The horizontal canopies define the continuous facade and give the building an organic quality and superb dynamism. Ministry of Education and Health, Rio de Janeiro, 1936-1943. This architectural statement by Le Corbusier was developed by Lucio Costa and Oscar Niemeyer and other colleagues.

Lacquer and cane easy chair designed by Niemeyer, seen in his office on Avenida Atlantica, Copacabana. Niemeyer sometimes uses the technique of pressing and molding wood. The forms and dimensions are varied in accordance with the specific needs of the object in order to achieve a simplicity that unites beauty and functionality.

Museum of Contemporary Art, Niterói, Brazil, 1991. Designed to house a fine collection of contemporary Brazilian art, this building constitutes an emblematic form, a beacon for people arriving in Rio de Janeiro from the sea. The museum is a revolutionary double curving figure in which the first and second floors are connected on the exterior by a ramp that also links the peripheral leisure and promenade areas to the more stable nucleus that will house the permanent collection.

Museum of Contemporary Art, Niterói, Brazil, 1991. One of Niemeyer's most attractive buildings, it is the most accomplished application of the interplay between solid and void, form and counterform, that he so abundantly and charismatically illustrated in his public buildings in Brazil.

Casa dos Canoas, Niemeyer's villa in Rio de Janeiro (São Conrado), 1952. In what is the last house he built for himself, Niemeyer emphasized the idea of the "free-form roof" with which he had earlier experimented in the Caso do Baile at Pampulha. Here he achieves a magical fusion of open and closed spaces that merges with the rocks, water and vegetation of its natural setting.

Casa dos Canoas, Niemeyer's villa in Rio de Janeiro (São Conrado), 1952. The transparency of the plan combines with chiaroscuro effects inside. The metal columns supporting the big concrete canopy roof never impede the light or the gaze as they move through the transparent skin that surrounds much of the building.

Memorial to Latin America, São Paulo, Brazil, 1986–1988. In the center of São Paulo, an area with few noteworthy buildings, the Memorial complex acts as a landmark. Here, the cubic volumes of the Institute of Latin America seem to be levitating as a result of the double rows of wires and columns used on the sides and at the back. As in the Memorial complex, formal perfection is the result of innovation.

Memorial to Latin America, São Paulo, Brazil, 1986–1988. The desire for unity in the Memorial project is expressed in the pedestrian bridge that links the different parts of the complex both physically and symbolically.
National Congress, Brasilia, 1958–1960. The two cupolas: in the foreground, the National Assembly, and behind, the Senate.

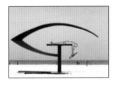

Copacabana beach, Rio de Janeiro, 2000. Niemeyer is also a sculptor, as can be seen from his recent works for Copacabana, whose combination of sea and sky forms what is still his favorite landscape.

Parliament of Latin America, São Paulo, 1991–1992. Part of the Memorial complex, the Parliament was inaugurated in 1992. The glass skin gives a poetic feel to this totally enclosed concrete structure. The white, graceful canopy has a sculptural quality, standing away from and lightening the building's curved surface.

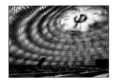

Headquarters of the French Communist Party, Paris (Place Colonel Fabien), France, 1967–1981. Niemeyer received the commission for this project during his second visit to France in 1965. The cupola and dome are two of the most highly evocative architectural forms and, because of their rich symbolism, should be used sparingly. Niemeyer therefore includes them in an exceptional complex, as he did ten years earlier for the National Congress building in Brasilia.

Copacabana, Rio de Janeiro, November 2000. Oscar Niemeyer with some of his "carioca" friends. "What really matters is not architecture, it is life and friends and this unjust world that we need to change." (Maxim written by Niemeyer on the wall of his office.)

Some of Niemeyer's photos, Rio de Janeiro, Brazil, November 2000.
Oscar Niemeyer in November 2000, Copacabana, Rio de Janeiro, Brazil. In addition to designing an infinite variety of buildings, Niemeyer has found time to write several books, to sculpt and to help the many museums that have paid tribute to this work. He still goes to his office every day to attend to ongoing projects.

The author dedicates this book to the memory of his father, Jean-Claude Salvaing.

The author and publisher would like to thank Oscar Niemeyer for his precious collaboration. Their gratitude also goes to Ana Lucia Niemeyer, Fernanda Martins, the Fundacaõ Oscar Niemeyer, the journalist Fritz Utzeri, the *Jornal do Brasil*, and the headquarters of the French Communist Party for their help in preparing this book.